Quick Revision

KS3

Maths

Hilary Koll and
Steve Mills

First published 2007
exclusively for WHSmith by
Hodder Murray, a member of the Hodder Headline group
338 Euston Road
London
NW1 3BH

Impression number 10 9 8 7 6 5 4 3 2 1
Year 2010 2009 2008 2007

A CIP record for this book is available from the British Library.

The right of Steve Mills and Hilary Koll to be identified as the authors of this work has been asserted by them.

Cover illustration by Sally Newton Illustrations.

Typeset by Starfish Design Editorial and Project Management Ltd.

ISBN: 978 0 340 94306 9

Printed and bound in the UK by Hobbs the Printers Ltd.

Algebraic expressions

Combining and simplifying expressions
Firstly, if necessary, open any brackets (expand).

E.g. $b + t + t + 2(1 + t) + 3(b + 2)$

$= b + t + t + 2 + 2t + 3b + 6$

Collect together all the terms that are the same. Treat terms containing letters, e.g. t and $3b$, separately from numbers on their own, e.g. 6 and 2.

E.g. $b + t + t + 2 + 2t + 3b + 6$
$= 4b + 4t + 8$

If you can, put any brackets back in to simplify further.

E.g. $4b + 4t + 8$
$= 4(b + t + 2)$

SEE ALSO Brackets, Factorising

Angles

Make sure you know how angles are related, in shapes and along lines.

- **Learn which angles are equal**

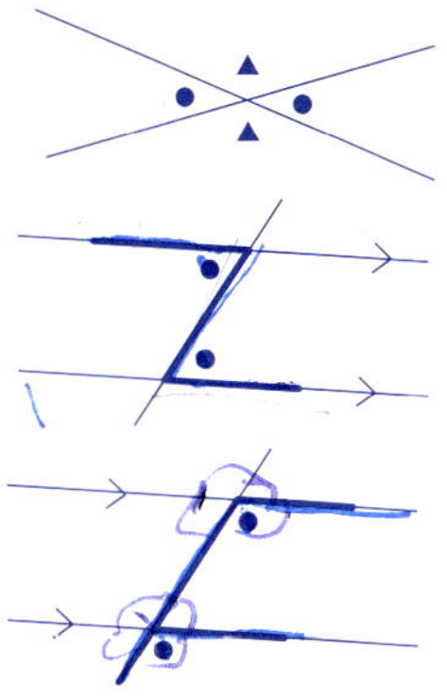

When two lines cross,
the **opposite angles** are **equal**.
• = • and ▲ = ▲

When a line crosses two parallel lines,
the angles in a 'Z' shape are **equal**.
• = • (called **alternate angles**)

When a line crosses two parallel lines,
the angles in an 'F' shape are **equal**.
• = • (called **corresponding angles**)

Remember: these shapes might be rotated or reflected!

Continued overleaf

- **Learn which angles total 180°**

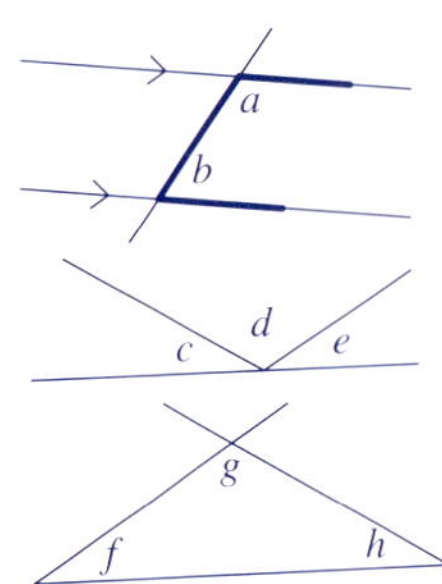

When a line crosses two parallel lines, the angles in a 'C' or 'U' shape total 180°. $a + b = 180°$ (called **interior angles**)

When angles form a straight line, they total 180°. $c + d + e = 180°$

When lines make a triangle, the angles inside the triangle total 180°. $f + g + h = 180°$

- **Learn which angles total 360°**

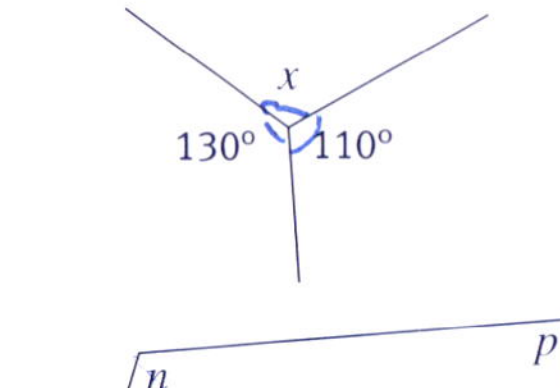

When angles are around a point, the angles total 360° . Use subtraction to find missing angle! $x = 360° - 110° - 130° = 120°$

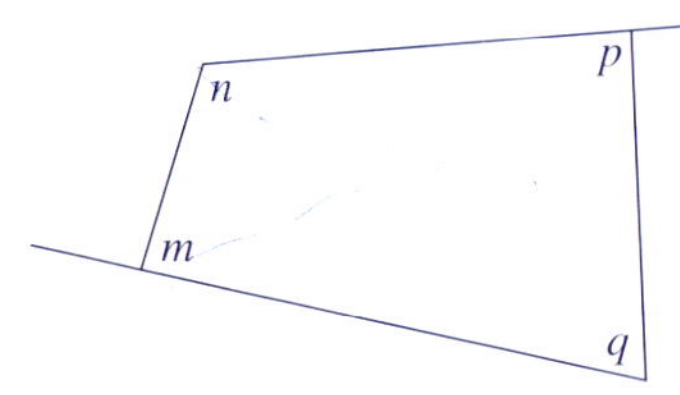

When lines make a quadrilateral, the angles inside total 180°. $m + n + p + q = 180°$

EXAM TIP

Write in *all* the angles you can find. One may help you find the answer.

SEE ALSO Parallel, Regular polygons, Interior and exterior angles

Approximation

We can change parts of a calculation to make it easier to do. For example, if the question is **8.2 × 19.67**, we can round the numbers to make **8 × 20**. The answer of 160 is an approximation of the real answer which is 161.294. This can help you to get an idea of what the real answer might be before calculating, to avoid silly answers.

SEE ALSO Rounding

Area

Area is the amount of surface that a 2D shape covers.

When finding areas of 2D shapes, use these formulae:

- Area of a rectangle = length × width

  $A = l \times w$

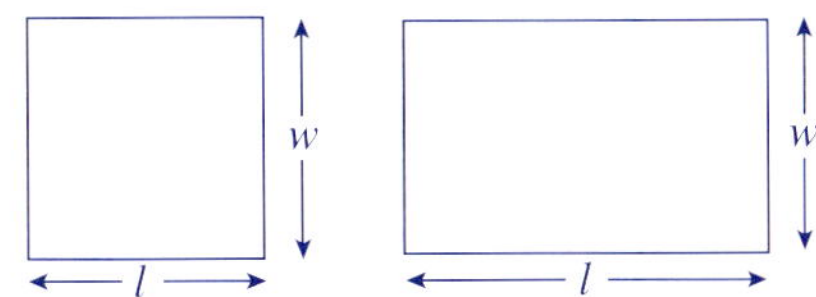

- Area of a triangle = $\frac{1}{2}$ base × perpendicular height

  $A = \frac{1}{2} \times b \times h$

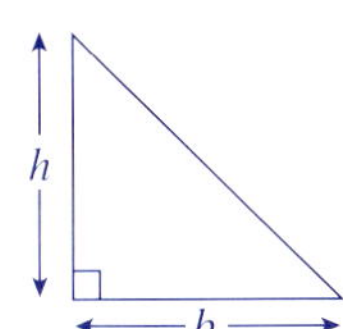

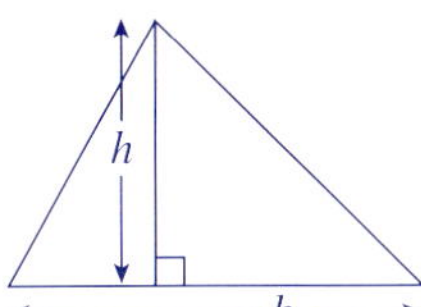

- Area of a trapezium = average of parallel sides × perpendicular height

  $A = \frac{a + b}{2} \times h$

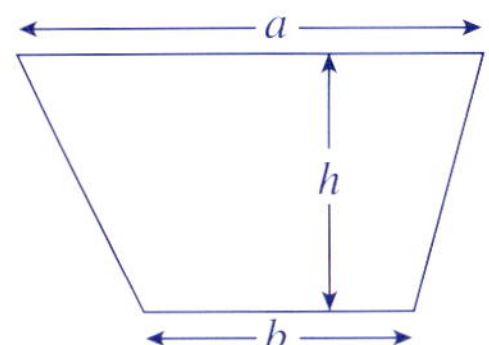

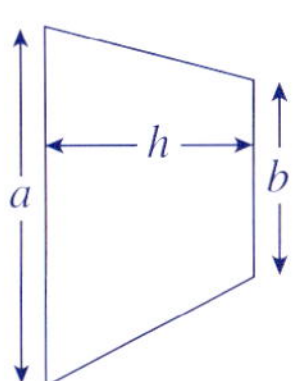

- Area of a parallelogram = base × perpendicular height

  $A = b \times h$

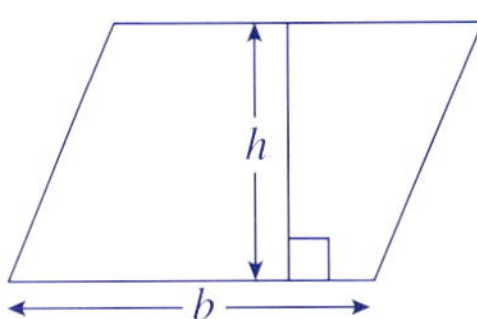

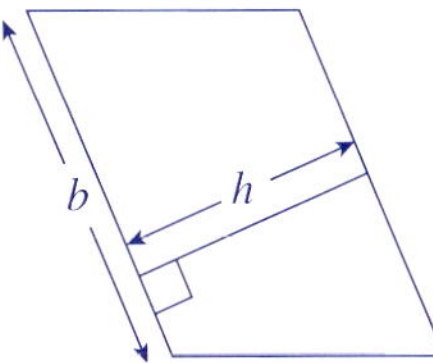

EXAM TIP

Remember that areas are generally written in cm^2 or m^2.

SEE ALSO Circles, Formula

Averages

There are three types of average: mode, median and mean.
E.g. Jo's scores at the bowling alley were 7, 2, 4, 7 and 5.

- **Mode:** the mode (or modal value) is the most popular or frequent value.
  E.g. **7**, 2, 4, **7**, 5 The mode is **7**.
  Note: there can be more than one mode.
- **Median:** the median is the middle value when the numbers are put in order.
  E.g. 7, 2, 4, 7, 5 → 2, 4, **5**, 7, 7 The median is **5**.
  If there is no middle value because there is an even number of scores, the median is halfway between the two middle values.
  E.g. the median of 2, 6, 8, 9 is **7**.
- **Mean:** to find the mean, we add the scores and divide the total by the number of scores.
  E.g. 7 + 2 + 4 + 7 + 5 = 25, so 25 ÷ 5 The mean is **5**.

SEE ALSO Range

Bar graphs

The information in this frequency table has been made into a bar graph. The times of goals have been grouped into equal class intervals of 15 minutes.

Times of goals scored (minutes)	Frequency
$0 \le t < 15$	8
$15 \le t < 30$	5
$30 \le t < 45$	7
$45 \le t < 60$	3
$60 \le t < 75$	11
$75 \le t < 90$	16

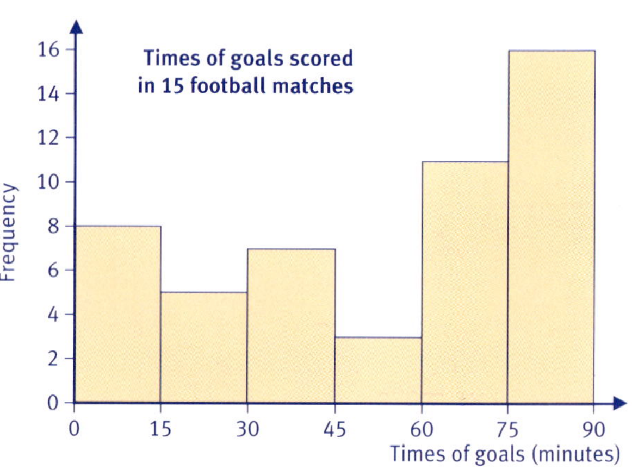

SEE ALSO Class intervals, Frequency table

Brackets

In calculations, brackets are used to show which part to work out first.

E.g. $3 \times (4 + 1) = 3 \times 5 = 15$

Without the brackets, the answer would be 13!

$3 \times 4 + 1 = 12 + 1 = 13$

In algebra, brackets are used to group things together.

Removing or opening brackets (expanding)

Multiply the term outside the brackets by each term inside the brackets.

E.g. $5\,(2y + 3) = 5 \times 2y + 5 \times 3 = 10y + 15$

When two brackets are side by side, the $\times$ sign has been left out.

$(2y + 3)\,(5y - 4)$ means $(2y + 3) \times (5y - 4)$

Draw lines to help you multiply the brackets, like this:

$(2y + 3)\,(5y - 4) = (2y \times 5y) + (3 \times -4) + (2y \times -4) + (3 \times 5y)$

$= 10y^2 - 12 - 8y + 15y$ (Collect like terms)

$= 10y^2 + 7y - 12$

Remember: two eyebrows, a nose and a mouth!

Putting in brackets (factorising)

This is the opposite of expanding. Look for common factors that can be taken outside the brackets.

$20y + 15$ ← Look for common factors! 5 is a factor of $20y$ and of 15.

$= 5(4y + 3)$

SEE ALSO Factors, Factorising

Capacity

Capacity is how much liquid a container can hold.
It generally is measured in millilitres or litres.
1000 millilitres make 1 litre 1000 ml = 1 l
There is a link between capacity and volume:
1 ml of water takes up 1 cm^3 of space.

SEE ALSO Volume

Circles

There are mathematical words and relationships you need to know about circles:

1 The **radius** of a circle is the distance from the centre to the edge.

2 The **diameter** is the distance across the circle through the centre. It is twice the length of the radius.
$d = 2r$

3 **Pi** (π) is the relationship between the circumference of a circle and its diameter. The circumference is always about 3.14 times longer than the diameter, i.e. π is approximately 3.14.

4 The circumference is the distance around a circle.
Circumference = $\pi \times$ diameter
$C = \pi d$ (also expressed as $C = 2\pi r$)

5 The area of a circle = $\pi \times$ radius^2
$A = \pi r^2$

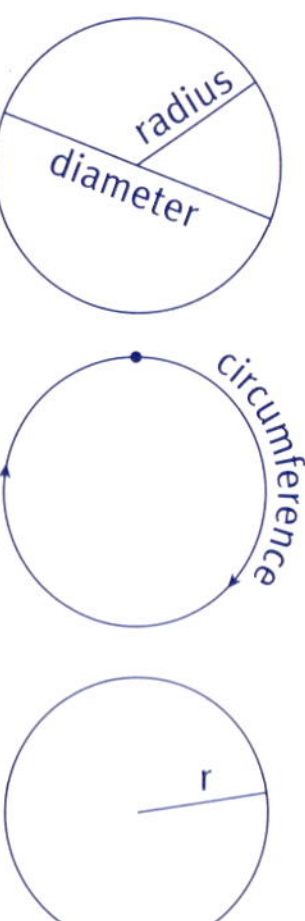

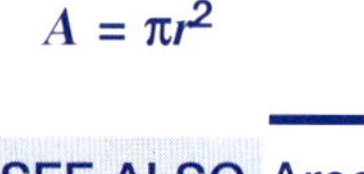

SEE ALSO Area

Class intervals

A class interval is the group size we use to help us to organise data more clearly. E.g. the ages of people under 50 using a Leisure Centre one lunchtime have been collected as a list:

6	**37**	**19**	**23**	**8**	**32**	**44**	**35**
43	**36**	**16**	**19**	**37**	**17**	**13**	**16**

We can arrange the data into equal class intervals.

Age group (class intervals)	Number of people
0–9	2
10–19	6
20–29	1
30–39	5
40–49	2

- Each class interval must be the same size.
- Class intervals are sometimes written using ≤ and < signs, so in the example, if a stands for the age, the table would read:

$$0 \leq a < 9$$
$$10 \leq a < 19 \quad \text{etc.}$$

SEE ALSO Bar graphs

Common denominator

Fractions have a common denominator when the denominator is the same.

E.g. $\frac{3}{8}$ and $\frac{5}{8}$

When adding and subtracting fractions, make sure the denominators are the same.

E.g. $\frac{3}{4} + \frac{4}{5}$

Change each fraction to an equivalent fraction so that the denominators are the same.

$\frac{15}{20} + \frac{16}{20} = \frac{31}{20} = 1\frac{11}{20}$

SEE ALSO Equivalent fractions, Fractions

Congruence

Shapes are congruent if they are the same shape and size as each other. They can be reflected or rotated but are still congruent.

These rectangles are congruent. These shapes are congruent.

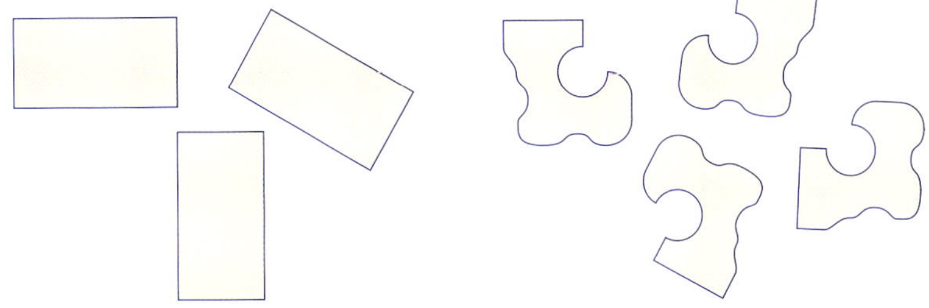

Conversion graphs

Conversion graphs help us to convert measurements in one unit into another. E.g.

To find how far 40 km is in miles, read across from 40 km to the diagonal line. Now read down to find the number of miles: 40 km = 25 miles

To find how far 50 miles is in kilometres, read up and then across: 50 miles = 80 km

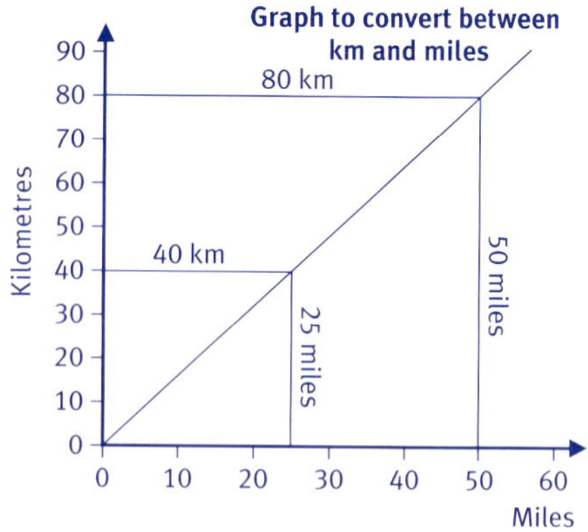

EXAM TIP

Use a ruler to make sure your lines are vertical and horizontal.

Co-ordinates

Co-ordinates are used to pinpoint exactly where a point is on a graph or map. The x (horizontal) co-ordinate is always given first.

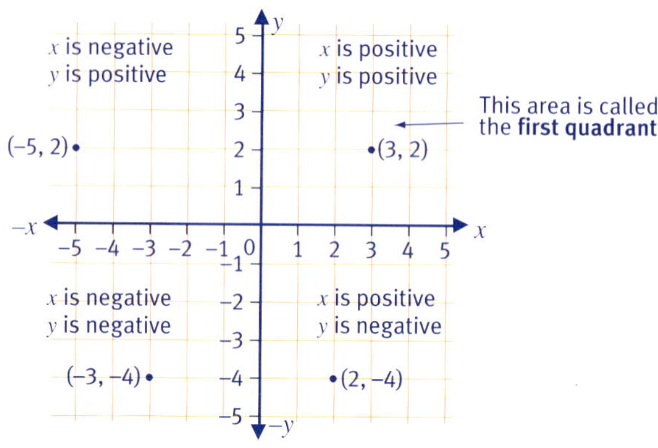

EXAM TIP

Remember: x is across (x is a cross!).

Cube numbers

Cube numbers (sometimes called cubed or cubic numbers) are made by multiplying one number by itself and by itself again.

E.g.	$1 \times 1 \times 1$	$2 \times 2 \times 2$	$3 \times 3 \times 3$	$4 \times 4 \times 4$	$5 \times 5 \times 5$	$6 \times 6 \times 6$
	1	**8**	**27**	**64**	**125**	**216 ...**

They are called cube numbers because they are the sequence of volumes of cubes.
E.g.

1 cm^3

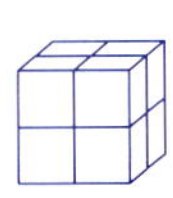

8 cm^3

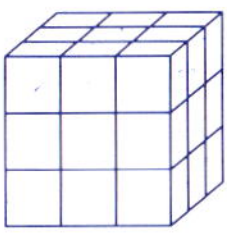

27 cm^3

SEE ALSO Square numbers, Sequences, *n*th term

Decimals

- **To change a decimal to a fraction**
  Make sure you know what the columns to the right of the decimal point stand for:

  tenths, hundredths, thousandths

  0.2 7 5

1 Look at the column furthest to the right of the decimal.

0.6 is 6 **tenths**, so we write this as the fraction $\frac{6}{10}$.

0.35 is 35 **hundredths**, so we write this as the fraction $\frac{35}{100}$.

0.275 is 275 **thousandths**, so we write this as the fraction $\frac{275}{1000}$.

2 If you can, change each fraction to its simplest form (cancel), by dividing the numerator and denominator by the same number.

$\frac{6}{10} = \frac{3}{5}$ (÷ 2, ÷ 2) $\quad \frac{35}{100} = \frac{7}{20}$ (÷ 5, ÷ 5) $\quad \frac{275}{1000} = \frac{11}{40}$ (÷25, ÷25)

Continued overleaf

- **To change a decimal to a percentage**
  Just multiply by 100!
  E.g. 0.25 as a percentage is $0.25 \times 100 = 25\%$
  0.175 as a percentage is $0.175 \times 100 = 17.5\%$

SEE ALSO Fractions, Percentages

Decimal places

The number of decimal places is the number of digits to the right of the decimal point.
E.g. 6.**39** has 2 decimal places and 13.**063** has 3 decimal places.

To round a number to 2 decimal places

1 Underline the important digit (the second decimal place).
26.5$\underline{7}$342 4.5$\underline{1}$64

2 Now look at the digit to the right of this.
26.5$\underline{7}$**3**42 4.5$\underline{1}$**6**4

- If it is below five, write the number as it stands with two decimal places.
  26.5$\underline{7}$**3**42 is 26.57 to 2 decimal places
- If it is five or more, round up.
  4.5$\underline{1}$**6**4 is 4.52 to 2 decimal places

Work in the same way when writing numbers to 1 or 3 decimal places. Always look at the digit to the right of the number of places you need.

SEE ALSO Rounding, Significant figures

Degrees

Degrees (°) are used to:

- show temperatures, e.g. 18°C
- show the size of an angle, e.g.

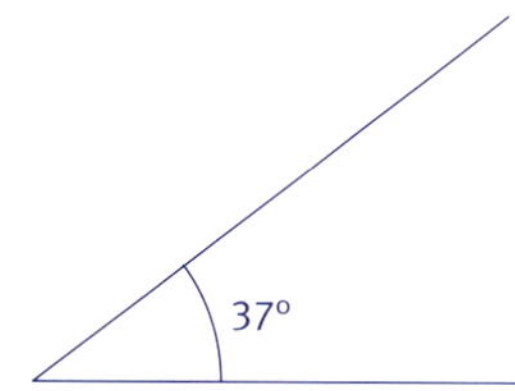

SEE ALSO Angles

Distance, speed and time

There is a relationship between distance, average speed and time.
If you know two of these measurements you can always find the third.
This relationship can be written in three ways:

1 Total distance = average speed × total time

$D = S \times T$

2 Average speed = total distance ÷ total time

$S = D \div T$ **or** $S = \dfrac{D}{T}$

3 Total time = total distance ÷ average speed

$T = D \div S$ **or** $T = \dfrac{D}{S}$

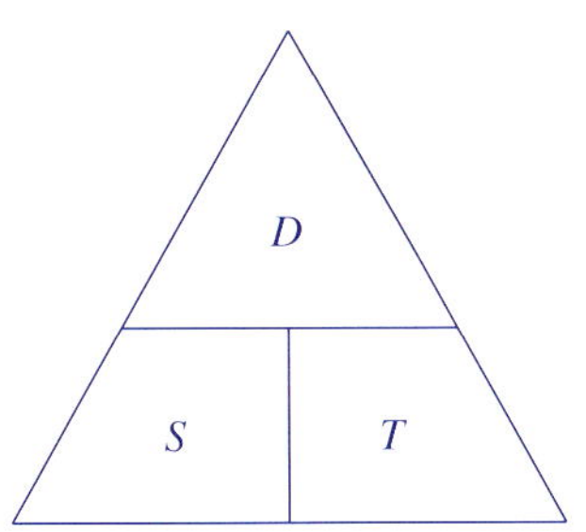

E.g. If a car travels 160 miles (D) in 5 hours (T), the average speed (S) is:

$S = D \div T$

$= 160 \div 5 = 32$ m.p.h.

EXAM TIP

On a distance–time graph, average speed can be found by finding the gradient.

SEE ALSO Gradient

Division

When dividing make sure your answer makes sense!

E.g. A coach can take 36 people.
How many coaches are needed to take 117 people on a trip?

$$36 \overline{)117} = 3.25$$

The answer to the question is *not* 3.25 coaches.
We must **round up** to 4 for it to make sense.

E.g. How many 26p stamps can I buy for £4.29?

$$26 \overline{)429} = 16.5$$

The answer to the question is *not* 16.5 stamps.
We must **round down** to 16 for it to make sense.

Equations

An equation is a true statement that contains an equals sign.

E.g. $7 + 3 = 10$ $4y = 10 - 2$ $x - 3 = 5y + 2$

Equations where no letter is raised to the power of 2 or higher are called **linear equations**.

E.g. $x + 2 = 9$ $4y - x + 2 = 0$ $r + 7 + 2t = 8$

Equations that have a letter to the power of 2 (squared) are called **quadratic equations**.

E.g. $x^2 + 2 = 9$ $4y^2 - y + 2 = 0$ $2t^2 + t = 8$

SEE ALSO Linear equations, Quadratic equations, Simultaneous equations

Equivalent fractions

Equivalent fractions have the same value even though they have different numerators and denominators.

E.g.

numerator → $\frac{3}{4} = \frac{9}{12} = \frac{12}{16}$ These three fractions are all equivalent.

denominator

Multiplying or dividing both the numerator and denominator of a fraction by the same number will create equivalent fractions.

E.g. $\frac{2}{5} = \frac{10}{25}$ (× 5 on top and bottom)

$\frac{54}{60} = \frac{27}{30} = \frac{9}{10}$ (÷ 2, then ÷ 3 on top and bottom) ← in its simplest form

To create the equivalent fraction in its **simplest form** (or **lowest terms**), divide by common factors until you can't divide any more.

SEE ALSO Factors, Common denominator, Fractions

Factors

Factors are whole numbers that divide exactly into another number.

E.g. Find all the factors of 24.

Look for factors in pairs. Work through from 1, trying each number in turn.

1 × **24** = 24
2 × **12** = 24
3 × **8** = 24
4 × **6** = 24
5 is not a factor of 24.
6 Stop when a number appears in the list again.

The factors of 24 are: 1, 2, 3, 4, 6, 8, 12 and 24.

EXAM TIP

Remember, if a number is an odd number it will have no even factors!

Factorising

Factorising is the opposite of expanding or opening brackets. Try to put in brackets, if you can, and look for factors that can be taken outside the brackets.

E.g.

$12n + 15$
$= 3(4n + 5)$

Look for common factors!
3 is a factor of $12n$ and of 15.

Always check your answer by multiplying out again.

$3(4n + 5) = \quad 3 \times 4n + 3 \times 5 \quad = \quad 12n + 15$ Correct!

SEE ALSO Factors, Brackets

Foreign currency

The exchange rate in the UK shows how much of another currency you get for £1.

Exchange rates

£1 = 1.62 US dollars

= 1.44 euros

E.g.

To find how many US dollars are the same as £8:

Multiply 8 by 1.62 (exchange rate) = $12.96.

To find how many pounds are the same as 360 euros

Divide 360 by 1.44 (exchange rate) = £250.

EXAM TIP

Remember, if exchange rate given as above:

Pounds → Other currency	*Multiply* by exchange rate
Other currency → Pounds	*Divide* by exchange rate

Formula

A formula is a general rule to help you see relationships between things. It can be written in words or with letters.

E.g. The formula for the area of a rectangle is length × width

or $A = l \times w$

Substituting

To use a formula to find an answer to a question, substitute the values you have been given for the words or letters in the formula.

E.g.

For a rectangle You have been told: length (l) = 10 cm

width (w) = 4 cm

You must find: area (A) = ?

$A = l \times w$

10 4 Substitute the given values for the letters.

$A = 10 \times 4$ Work out the answer!

$A = 40\text{ cm}^2$

Always think carefully about the unit of your answer. Area is usually cm^2.

Rearranging a formula

Sometimes the formula needs to be rearranged to help you find an answer. E.g.

For a rectangle You have been told: area (A) = 30 cm^2
width (w) = 5 cm
You must find: length (l) = ?

Rearrange the formula so that the length (l) is on one side of the equals sign and the other letters are on the other side.

$$A = l \times w$$

Do the opposite!
Divide both sides by w.

$$A \div w = l \times w \div w$$
$$A \div w = l$$

Now you can substitute the values: $30 \div 5 = l$, so $l = 6$ cm.

SEE ALSO Linear equations, Area

Fractions

Make sure you know these fraction words:

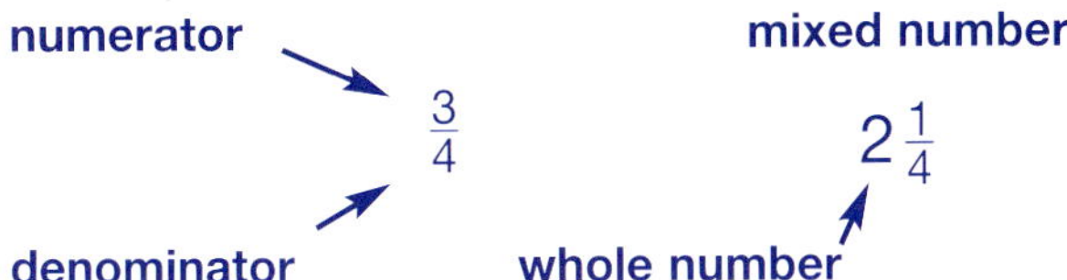

Mixed numbers → Improper fractions

E.g. Change $2\frac{1}{4}$ to an improper fraction.

- Look at the denominator. 4
- Multiply the whole number by this. $2 \times 4 = 8$
- Add the numerator. $8 + 1 = 9$

This is the new numerator. → 9
The denominator stays the same. → 4

$$\frac{9}{4}$$

Continued overleaf

Improper fractions → Mixed numbers

E.g. Change $\frac{13}{5}$ to a mixed number.

- Divide numerator by denominator. *How many 5s are in 13?*
  $13 \div 5 = 2$ remainder 3

  Write this as:

  $2\frac{3}{5}$ ← denominator is the same

Adding and subtracting fractions

When adding and subtracting fractions, make sure the denominators are the same.

E.g.

$\frac{3}{4} + \frac{4}{5}$

Change each fraction to an equivalent fraction so that the denominators are the same.

$\frac{15}{20} + \frac{16}{20}$

Add or subtract **only** the numerators. The denominator stays the same!

$= \frac{31}{20} = 1\frac{11}{20}$

Multiplying and dividing fractions

Multiply numerator by numerator and denominator by denominator.

E.g.

$$\frac{9}{4} \times \frac{2}{5} = \frac{18}{20} = \frac{9}{10}$$

To divide, turn the second fraction upside down and multiply!

E.g. $\frac{9}{4} \div \frac{3}{5} = \frac{9}{4} \times \frac{5}{3} = \frac{45}{12} = \frac{15}{4} = 3\frac{3}{4}$

To change a fraction to a decimal

Use a calculator to divide the numerator by the denominator.

SEE ALSO Common denominator, Decimals, Equivalent fractions

Frequency table

The frequency of an event is the number of times it occurs.
A frequency table shows this information for several events, sometimes using tallying.
E.g. This table shows that the flavour most frequently picked is Cheese.

Favourite Crisp Flavours		
Flavour	**Tally**	**Total**
Plain	|||	3
Cheese	~~||||~~ |||	8
Salt 'n vinegar	||	2
Prawn	~~||||~~	5
Bacon	~~||||~~ |	6

Gradient

A gradient is the slope of a line. We can calculate it using this formula:

Gradient = $\dfrac{\textbf{vertical distance}}{\textbf{horizontal distance}}$

E.g.

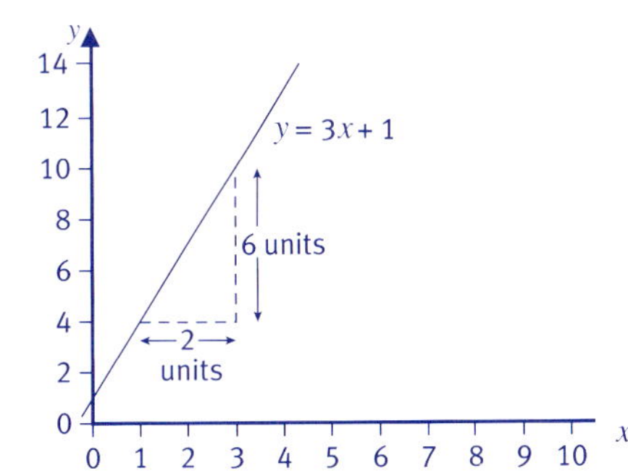

Gradient = $\frac{6}{2}$ = 3 (or +3)

This is a **positive** gradient as the line slants diagonally up towards the **right**.
Gradients are **negative** if the lines slope up towards the **left**.

Gradients can also be found using the equation of the line:

E.g. $y = \mathbf{3}x + 4$ has a gradient of **3**.
$y = \mathbf{-2}x + 5$ has a gradient of **–2**.

Remember, in the general equation of a straight line $y = mx + c$, m is always the gradient and c is where the line crosses the y axis.

SEE ALSO Linear graphs

Imperial units

There are two types of units of measurement: metric and imperial. Here are some imperial units you should know.

Length
12 inches = 1 foot
3 feet = 1 yard
1760 yards = 1 mile

Mass
16 ounces = 1 pound
14 pounds = 1 stone

Capacity
8 pints = 1 gallon

Approximate equivalences between metric and imperial units:

1 inch ≈ 2.5 cm
1 mile ≈ 1.6 km
2.2 pounds ≈ 1 kg
1 gallon ≈ 4.5 l

Use these when converting between units.

E.g. 8 miles ≈ 8 × 1.6 ≈ 12.8 km
16 km ≈ 16 ÷ 1.6 ≈ 10 miles

EXAM TIP

Remember: miles → km *multiply* by 1.6
km → miles *divide* by 1.6
(1 mile > 1 km)

Index notation

5^4 means 5 to the power 4 and shows the number of 5s that have been multiplied together.

$5^4 = 5 \times 5 \times 5 \times 5$
$= 25 \times 25 = 625$

$6^3 = 6 \times 6 \times 6$
$= 36 \times 6 = 216$

$2^5 = 2 \times 2 \times 2 \times 2 \times 2$
$= 4 \times 4 \times 2$
$= 16 \times 2 = 32$

Multiplying and dividing indices

When multiplying with indices, **add** the powers.

E.g. 3 + 2 → 5

$4^3 \times 4^2 = (4 \times 4 \times 4) \times (4 \times 4) = 4^5$

When dividing with indices, **subtract** the powers.

E.g. 3 − 2 → 1

$4^3 \div 4^2 = \frac{(4 \times 4 \times 4)}{(4 \times 4)} = 4^1 = 4$

Interior and exterior angles

Remember: the exterior angles of any concave polygon add up to 360°.

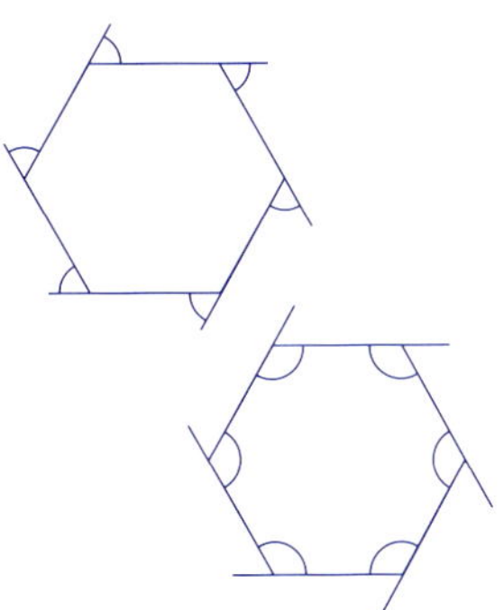

1 To find the size of each exterior angle of a **regular** polygon, divide 360° by the number of sides.
E.g. External angles of a regular hexagon
= 360° ÷ 6 = 60° each

2 To find the size of the interior angles, just subtract one of the exterior angles from 180°.
Internal angles of a regular hexagon
= 180° – 60° = 120° each

SEE ALSO Regular polygons, Angles

Length

Make sure you know the relationships between these metric units of length.
10 millimetres (mm) = 1 centimetre (cm)
100 centimetres (cm) = 1 metre (m)
1000 metres (m) = 1 kilometre (km)

SEE ALSO Metric units, Imperial units

Linear equations

A linear equation is a true statement with an equals sign, where no letter is raised to the power of 2 or higher.
E.g. $x + 2 = 9$ $4y = 10 - 2$ $x - 3 = 5y + 2$

Solving linear equations

1 Think of the equation as a pair of balance scales, with the = as the balancing point. What is on one side is equal to what is on the other.

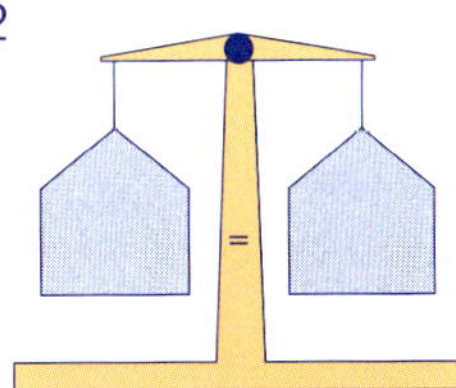

Continued overleaf

2 Try to rearrange the equation to get letters on one side and numbers on the other.
The scales will still balance if you do exactly the same to each side.
You can: **add** the same quantity to each side
subtract the same quantity from each side
multiply each side by the same quantity
divide each side by the same quantity.

E.g. To solve $\mathbf{5x - 4 = 26}$

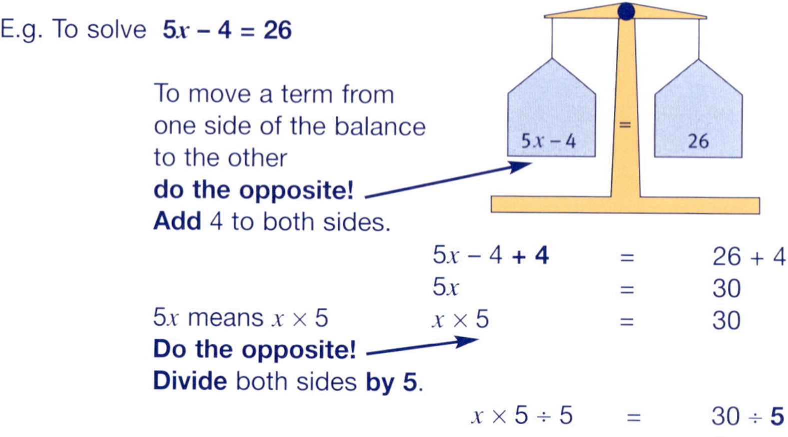

To move a term from one side of the balance to the other
do the opposite!
Add 4 to both sides.

$$5x - 4 \mathbf{+ 4} = 26 + 4$$
$$5x = 30$$

$5x$ means $x \times 5$

$$x \times 5 = 30$$

Do the opposite!
Divide both sides **by 5**.

$$x \times 5 \div 5 = 30 \div \mathbf{5}$$
$$\mathbf{x = 6}$$

EXAM TIP

Always put your answer back into the original equation as a check e.g. $5x - 4 = 26$. If $x = 6$ then $(5 \times 6) - 4 = 26$. Correct!

Linear graphs

A linear equation that includes x and y can be plotted to form a straight line on a graph. This is called a **straight-line** or **linear graph**.

- Use the equation to work out some of the values for x and y.
  E.g. $\mathbf{y = 2x + 1}$
  Draw a table and choose some simple values for x, like –2, –1, 0, 1, 2. (Always choose three or more values.)

x	–2	–1	0	1	2
$2x$	–4	–2	0	2	4
$y = 2x + 1$	–3	–1	1	3	5

- Now plot the values of x and y onto a suitable graph, and join the points with a straight line.

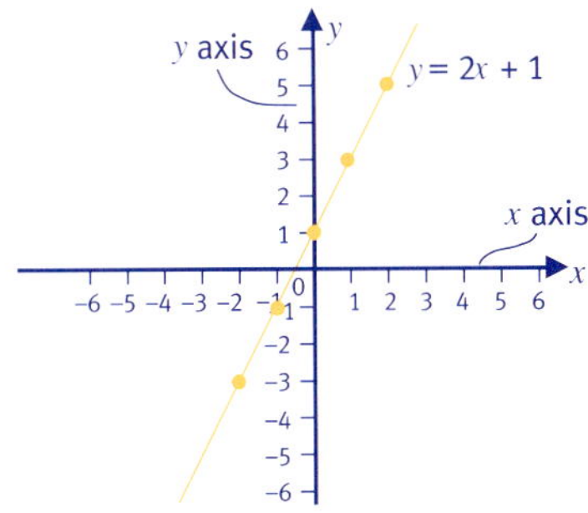

SEE ALSO Gradient, Linear equations

Line graphs

Line graphs show information by joining points up with lines.

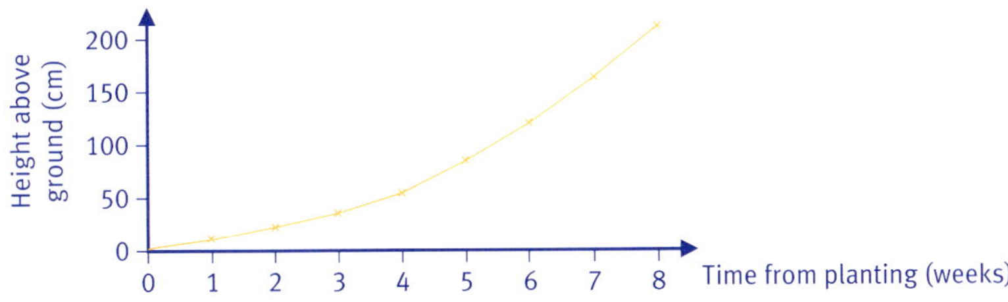

Sometimes the symbol ⦚ is used to show that some of the scale has been missed out.

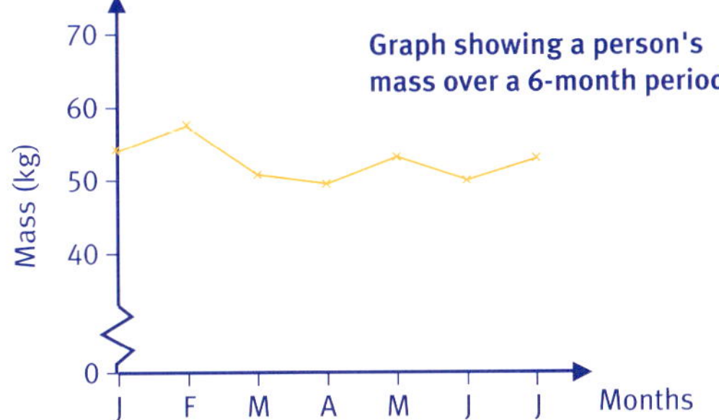

Lowest common multiple (LCM)

The lowest common multiple of 3, 4 and 5 is 60 because 60 is the lowest number that 3, 4 and 5 will all divide into exactly.

Mass

The mass of something is the amount of matter it is made from.
Mass differs from weight because the weight of something can change depending on where it is weighed. On the Moon a person weighs only one-sixth of their weight on Earth, but their mass remains the same.
Make sure you know the relationships between these metric units of mass:
1000 grams (g) = 1 kilogram (kg)
1000 kilograms (kg) = 1 tonne (t)

SEE ALSO Metric units, Imperial units, Weight

Metric units

Metric units are based on the number 10 and powers of 10, e.g. 1 m = 100 cm, 1 km = 1000 m, etc.
Metric units originated in France and are now used throughout Europe and in many other parts of the world.

SEE ALSO Capacity, Imperial units, Length, Mass

Multiples

A multiple of a number is any number into which it will divide exactly. Multiples of 6 are 6, 12, 18, ..., 66, ..., 348, ..., 600, etc.

SEE ALSO Lowest common multiple (LCM)

Multiplication

Multiplication questions such as 34 × 17 or 352 × 18 can be worked out using a grid method.

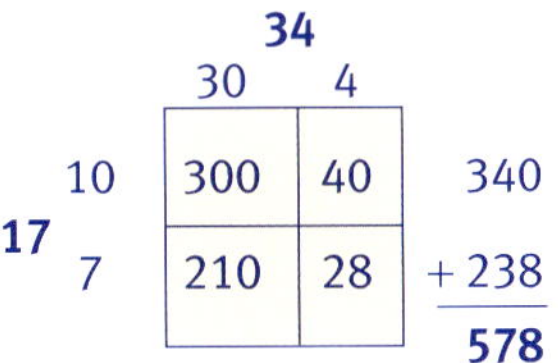

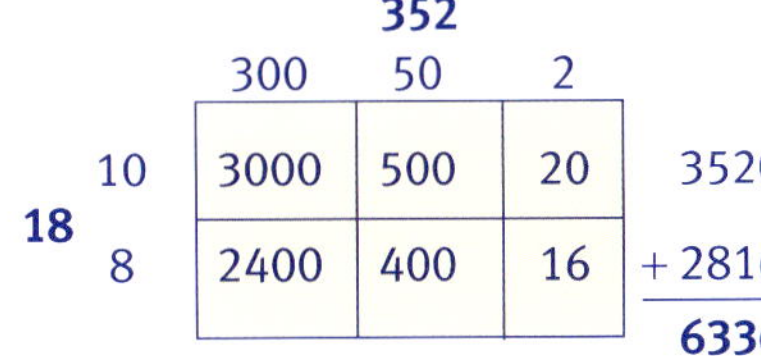

352
300 50 2
18
10 3000 500 20 3520
8 2400 400 16 + 2816
6336

Negative numbers

Negative numbers are those below zero, shown here on a number line.

−10 −9 −8 −7 −6 −5 −4 −3 −2 −1 0 1 2 3 4 5 6 7 8 9 10

negative numbers positive numbers

Positive numbers can be written with or without a '+' sign, e.g. 3 or +3.

Adding and subtracting

Use a number line to count on or back.

E.g. 4 − 9 + 3 = −2

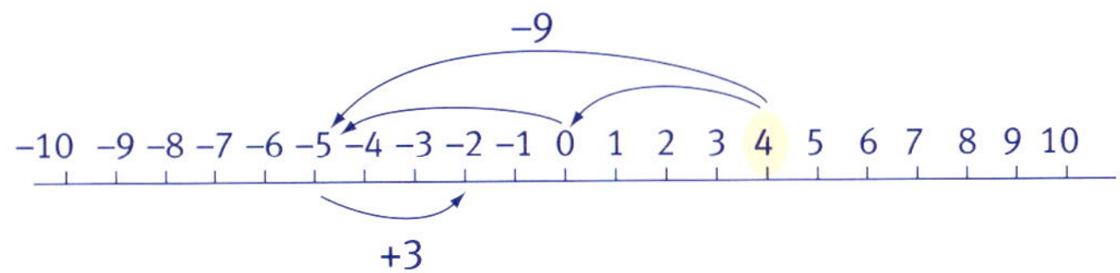

Multiplying and dividing with negative and positive numbers

These rules only apply to multiplication and division.

+	+	gives a positive (+) answer
+	−	gives a negative (−) answer
−	+	gives a negative (−) answer
−	−	gives a positive (+) answer

E.g. 3 × 4 = 12   3 × −4 = −12

−3 × 4 = −12   −3 × −4 = 12

Nets

A net is a 3D shape folded out flat. It shows the faces of the shape.

Cube **Cuboid** **Triangular prism** **Triangular-based pyramid**

EXAM TIP

Edges that join together are always the same length.

*n*th term

To find the *n*th term of a sequence, e.g. 2, 6, 10, 14, 18, …, follow steps 1 and 2:

1 First, look for the difference between each term.

If the difference is the same, multiply this number by n, e.g. $4n$, then…

2 Find the values for $4n$, where n is 1, 2, 3, …, etc. and compare this with your sequence:

Term	**1**	**2**	**3**	**4**	**5**
$4n$	4	8	12	16	20
sequence	2	6	10	14	18

This sequence is 2 less than $4n$ so the nth term is $\mathbf{4n - 2}$.

Note: If the differences are not the same, the sequence might show square numbers (n^2), cube numbers (n^3) or triangular numbers.

Here is the pattern of triangular numbers:

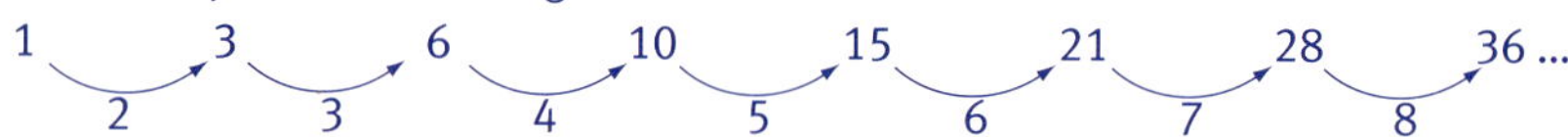

The rule for the nth term of this sequence is $\frac{1}{2}n\,(n + 1)$.

SEE ALSO Sequences

Parallel

Parallel lines are the same distance apart throughout their length.
These sets of lines are parallel.

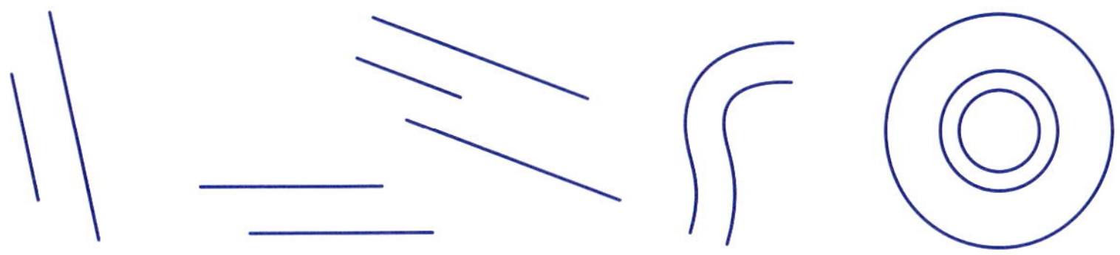

Quadrilaterals (four-sided shapes) made from two sets of parallel lines are called **parallelograms**.

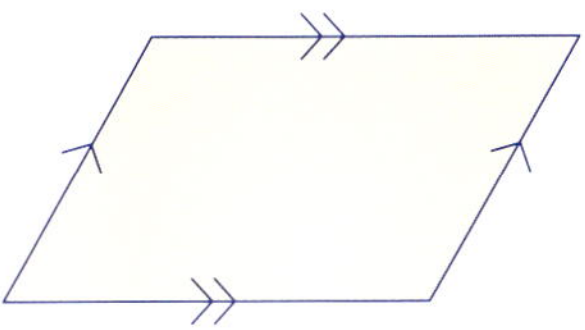

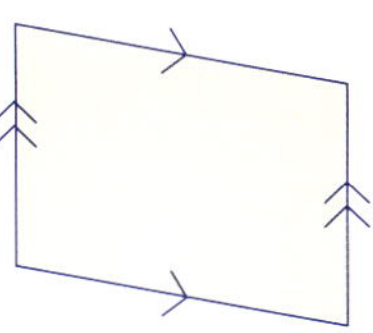

SEE ALSO Perpendicular, Angles

Percentages

Per cent means 'out of a hundred' or 'for every hundred'.

Think of a percentage such as 30% as the fraction $\frac{30}{100}$.

There are two types of percentage question:

1 When your answer will be a percentage

E.g. Jim scored 44 out of 80 in a test. What percentage is that?

Write the score as a fraction and multiply by 100 to find the percentage:

$\frac{44}{80} \times 100 = 55\%$

Continued overleaf

2 When your answer will be an amount

E.g. Find 30% of £60.

Write the percentage as a fraction and think of the word 'of' as a multiplication sign.

Find 30% of £60.

$\frac{30}{100} \times £60 = £18$ Use a calculator to find the answer.

You could also find this in your head:

- find 10% of £60 by dividing by 10;
- multiply by 3 to find 30%.

Questions asking you to find an increase or a discount (reduction, decrease) are of this type. You must remember to add to or subtract from your answer at the end.

E.g. A jumper costs £16. It is offered in a sale for 20% off. What is its sale price? First find 20% of £16.

$\frac{20}{100} \times £16 = £3.20$

Now subtract the discount from the original price: £16 – £3.20 = £12.80

SEE ALSO Fractions, Decimals

Perimeter

The perimeter of a shape is the distance around it.
The perimeter of a circle is called the circumference.
To find the perimeter of a rectangle, find the total of all the sides.
Notice that this is twice the length plus twice the width.

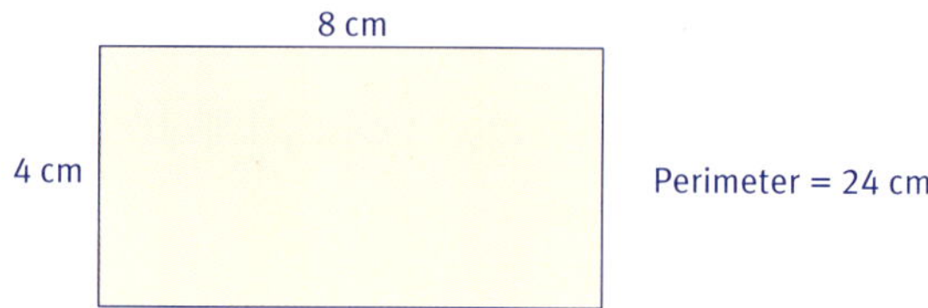

SEE ALSO Area, Circles

Perpendicular

A perpendicular line is one at right angles to another line.

The line AB is perpendicular to the line CD
and
the line CD is perpendicular to the line AB.

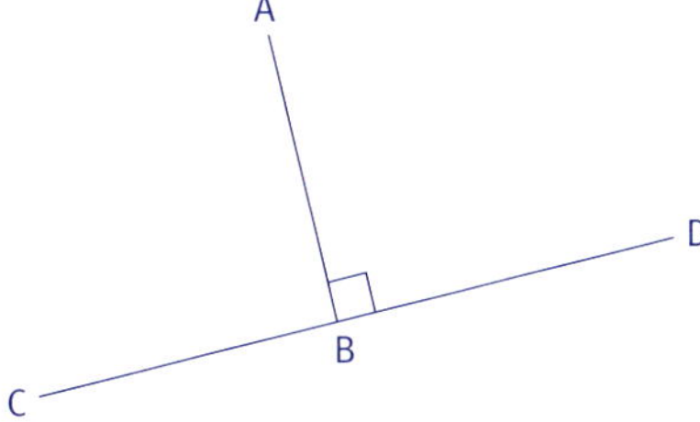

Pie chart

Pie charts show information by splitting a circle into sectors of different sizes. E.g. **24** people were asked where they went on holiday last year. Their answers are summarised in this frequency table:

Country	Frequency
France	5
Spain	7
Greece	3
Portugal	1
Britain	8

To draw a pie chart

1 Find the angle that each person (or unit) will take up, by dividing 360° by the total number.
E.g. 360° ÷ **24** = 15° per person.

2 Once you know how many degrees per person, you can multiply for each group of data, in this example each country.

Country	Number of People	Multiply	Angle
France	5	15° × 5	France = 75°
Spain	7	15° × 7	Spain = 105°
Greece	3	15° × 3	Greece = 45°
Portugal	1	15° × 1	Portugal = 15°
Britain	8	15° × 8	Britain = 120°
	24		Total = 360°

Continued overleaf

3 Now plot the pie chart using a protractor.

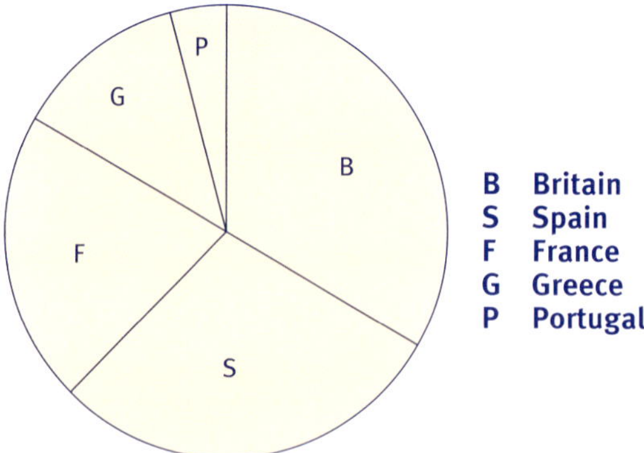

B **Britain**
S **Spain**
F **France**
G **Greece**
P **Portugal**

EXAM TIP

Always check that the total of your angles is 360°.

Polygons

Polygons are 2D (flat) shapes with straight sides.
Make sure you know the names of these shapes:

Shape name	Number of sides
triangle	3
quadrilateral	4
pentagon	5
hexagon	6
heptagon	7
octagon	8
nonagon	9
decagon	10

Remember that the sides of these shapes do not have to be the same length.

These shapes are all pentagons.

SEE ALSO Regular polygons, Quadrilaterals, Interior and exterior angles

Polyhedron

A polyhedron (plural: polyhedra) is a 3D shape with flat faces.

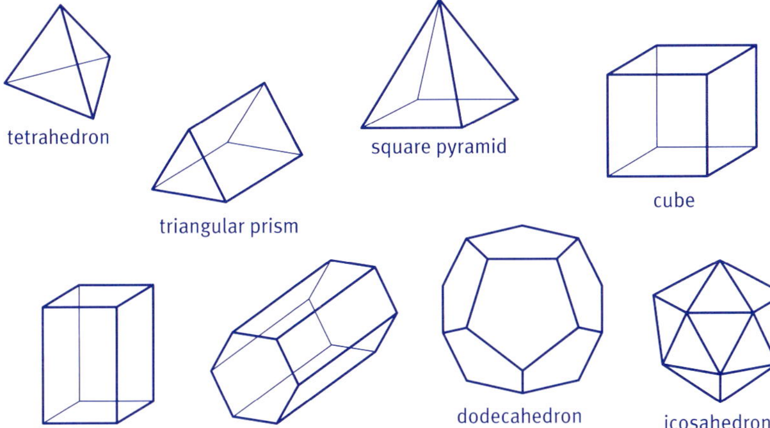

Prime numbers

A prime number has only two factors: itself and 1.
E.g.

7 is prime as it only has the factors 1 and 7.
6 is *not* prime as it has the factors 1, 2, 3 and 6.

The first ten prime numbers are:

2, 3, 5, 7, 11, 13, 17, 19, 23, 29.

Note: 2 is the only even prime number.

To check whether a 2-digit number is prime
Test to see if 2, 3, 5 or 7 is a factor of it.

	Factors?	
E.g. For 89	2	no (as 89 is odd)
	3	no
	5	no (as it doesn't end in 0 or 5)
	7	no

So 89 is prime.

SEE ALSO Factors

Probability

Probability is about the chance, or likelihood, of something happening. It can be marked on a scale from 0 to 1. Probabilities are written as fractions or decimals, e.g. $\frac{1}{4}$, 0.25.

impossible 0 — even chance — certain 1

We calculate probabilities like this:

$$\text{Probability of an event} = \frac{\text{number of ways this can happen}}{\text{number of equally likely outcomes}}$$

E.g. Probability of rolling the number four on a dice is $\frac{1}{6}$.

← only **1** number four on the dice

← **6** equally likely outcomes

SEE ALSO Tree diagrams

Pythagoras' Theorem

Pythagoras' Theorem is used to find the length of one side of a right-angled triangle, if given the other two sides.

Pythagoras' Theorem

$a^2 + b^2 = c^2$

c is the longest side, called the hypotenuse

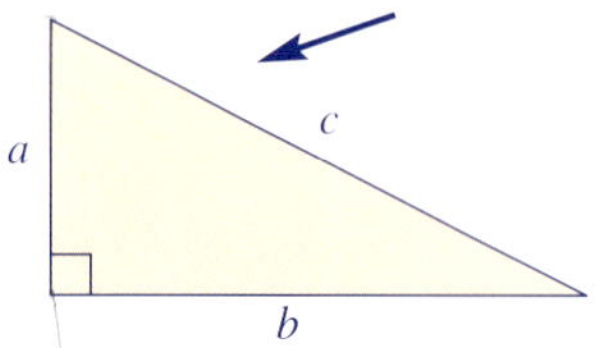

Find the length of the hypotenuse.

6cm

8cm

$a^2 + b^2 = c^2$

$6^2 + 8^2 = c^2$

$36 + 64 = c^2$

$100 = c^2$

$c = \sqrt{100}$ ← You can use the square root key √ on your calculator.

$c =$ 10 cm

SEE ALSO Square numbers, Squares and square roots

Quadratic equations

If an equation has a letter to the power of 2, it is called a quadratic equation.

E.g. $y = x^2 + 1$ or $x^2 + x - 2 = 0$

A quadratic expression is formed when multiplying two brackets like these:

$(y + 4)(y - 3)$

$$\begin{aligned}(y + 4)(y - 3) &= (y \times y) + (4 \times -3) + (y \times -3) + (4 \times y) \\ &= y^2 - 12 - 3y + 4y \quad \text{(Collect like terms.)} \\ &= y^2 + y - 12\end{aligned}$$

Remember: two eyebrows, a nose and a mouth!

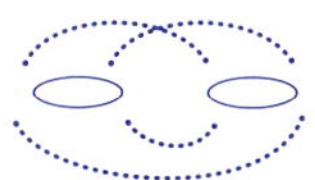

SEE ALSO Brackets, Equations, Linear equations, Trial and improvement

Quadrilaterals

Quadrilaterals are 2D shapes with four straight sides.
The interior angles of every quadrilateral add up to 360°.
Make sure you know about these special quadrilaterals:

Parallelogram
2 pairs of parallel sides
opposite sides equal
opposite angles equal

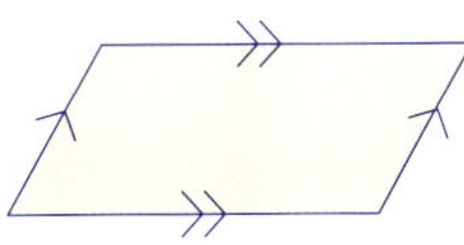

Rhombus
2 pairs of parallel sides
4 equal sides
opposite angles equal

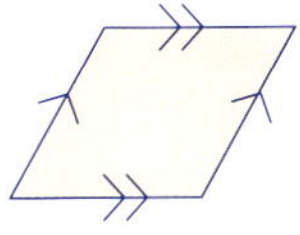

Rectangle
2 pairs of parallel sides
4 right angles

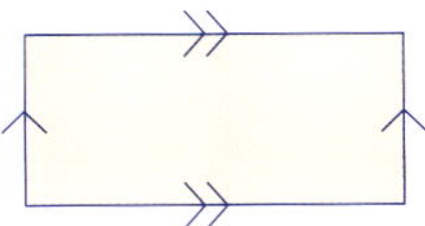

Trapezium
1 pair of parallel sides
no equal sides
no equal angles

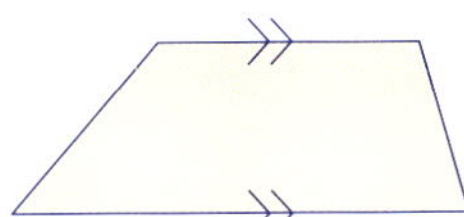

Continued overleaf

Isosceles trapezium
1 pair of parallel sides
2 pairs of equal angles
2 equal opposite sides

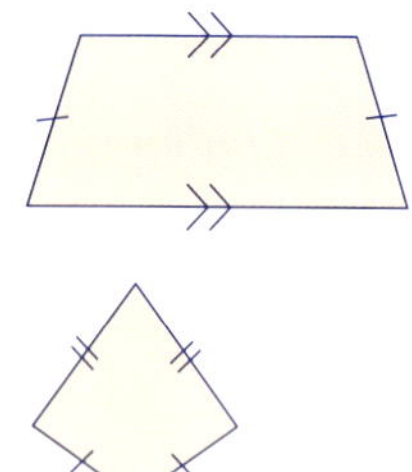

Kite
no parallel sides
2 pairs of equal sides
1 pair of equal angles

EXAM TIP

Many of these shapes are related, e.g. a square is a type of rectangle and rectangles and rhombuses are types of parallelograms.

Range

The range of a group of numbers is the **difference** between the largest and smallest numbers.

Find the range of these numbers: 3, 7, 6, 2, 9, 10, 4

Use subtraction! (smallest: 2, largest: 10)

Range = 10 – 2 = 8

SEE ALSO Averages

Ratio

Ratio is the relationship between two or more quantities or numbers. A shop says 'For every two bottles you buy, you get one free'. This can be written as the ratio 2:1.

However many times you buy two, you will always get one free.

2 : 1	
4 : 2	If I buy 4, I will get 2 free.
6 : 3	If I buy 6, I will get 3 free.
20:10	If I buy 20, I will get 10 free.

Notice that we can multiply both numbers in the ratio by any number and it is still the same relationship.

Q: *How many would you get free if you bought 12 bottles?*

$$\times 6 \left(\frac{2 : 1}{12 : ?} \right) \times 6$$

Answer = 6 free bottles

Q: *How many did I buy if I was given 8 bottles free?*

$$\times 8 \left(\frac{2 : 1}{? : 8} \right) \times 8$$

Answer = 16 bottles bought

Q: *How many did I buy and how many were free if I got 27 bottles altogether?*

Add the numbers in the ratio

$$\times 9 \left(\frac{2 : 1 = 3}{? : ? = 27} \right) \times 9$$

Answer = 18 bottles bought and 9 free

EXAM TIP

Check that they add to make the total number (in this example, 27).

Reflective symmetry

A 2D shape has reflective symmetry if it has one or more lines of symmetry (mirror lines).

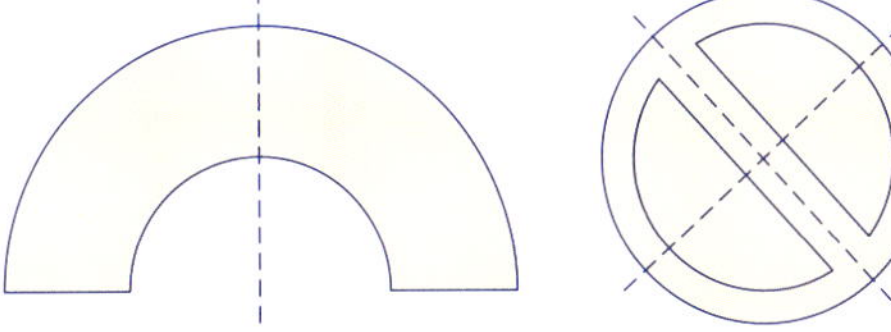

Remember that lines of symmetry might be in any direction and that there can be more than one.
A regular shape will have the same number of lines of symmetry as it has sides.

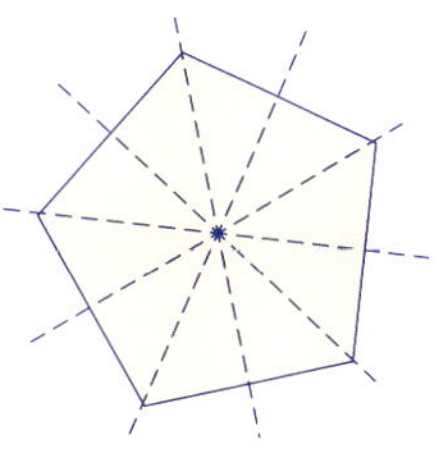

SEE ALSO Rotational symmetry

Regular polygons

If a polygon has sides of equal length *and* interior angles of equal size it is called a **regular** polygon. If not, it is an **irregular** polygon.

Note: A regular triangle is an equilateral triangle.
A regular quadrilateral is a square.

Here are some regular polygons:

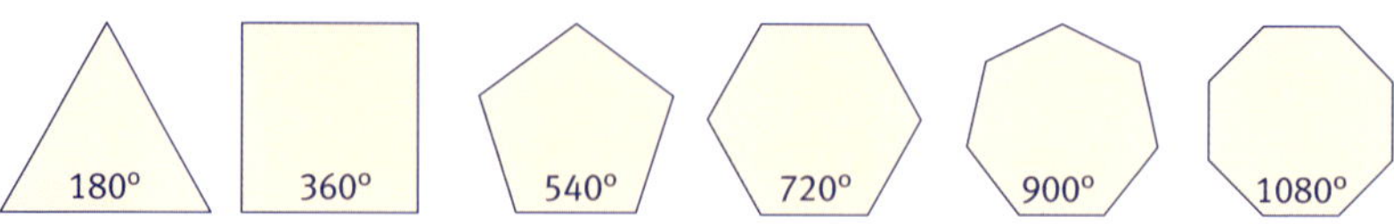

The number written in each shape shows the total of all the interior angles.
Can you see a pattern?
(Add 180° each time.)

Because the **interior angles** of a regular polygon are all the same, we can work out what size each is by dividing by the number of sides/angles.

180° ÷ 3 = 60° 360° ÷ 4 = 90° 540° ÷ 5 = 108°

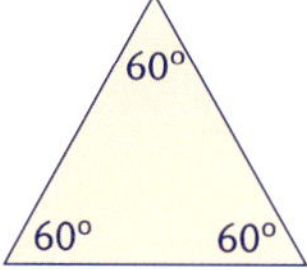

90° 90°

90° 90°

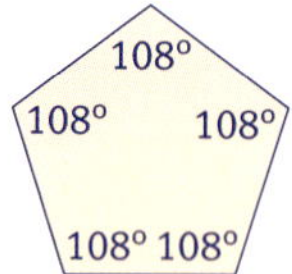

SEE ALSO Angles, Interior and exterior angles, Polygons

Rotational symmetry

The order of rotational symmetry a shape has is the number of ways it fits into its outline as it is rotated through 360°.

This shape has rotational symmetry of **order 5**.

This shape has rotational symmetry of **order 4**.

This shape has rotational symmetry of **order 1**.

SEE ALSO Reflective symmetry

Rounding

Numbers can be rounded in different ways.

E.g. **to** the nearest whole number
to the nearest ten or hundred
to 2 decimal places
to 3 significant figures, etc.

Rounding a number

1 Look at what you are rounding **to** and underline the important digit or digits in your number.
36 485.73 to 1 decimal place
36 485.73 to the nearest 10
36 485.73 to 3 significant figures

2 Now look at the next digit to the **right** of this.
If it is **below five**, write the number as it stands, up to your marked digit.
If it is **five or above**, round up.

E.g. below 5

36 485.7**3** to 1 decimal place is 36 485.7

5 or above

36 48**5**.73 to the nearest 10 is 36 490

5 or above

36 4**8**5.73 to 3 significant figures is 36 500

Remember to include zeros for columns up to the decimal point.

SEE ALSO Decimals, Decimal places, Significant figures

Scale factor

When enlarging a shape, a scale factor is needed to show how much larger to make the new shape.
Scale factor **3** means each side of the new shape should be **three times** longer than the same side of the original shape.
Scale factor **4** means each side of the new shape should be **four times** longer than the same side of the original shape, etc.
This rectangle has been enlarged by scale factor 2.
We say these two shapes are **similar** as they both have the same angles and have sides in the same ratio.

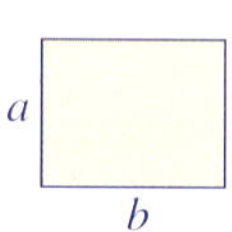

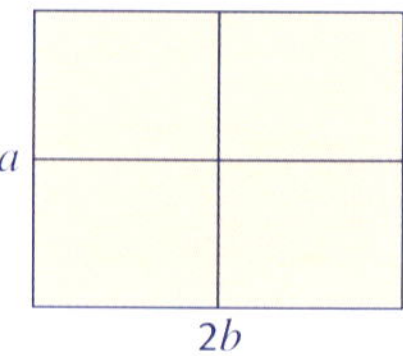

Note that the **area** of the new shape is **not** 2 times larger, but **4 times** (2×2) larger.

SEE ALSO Similarity

Scatter diagrams

Scatter graphs/diagrams show how closely two things are related to each other.

Positive correlation

(both values increase)

- People tend to buy more icecream in warmer weather.

Draw the **line of best fit** so that an equal number of crosses is on each side.

Negative correlation

(one value increases as the other decreases)

- The faster the car's speed, the less time is needed for the journey.

Zero correlation

- There is no link between your intelligence and the length of your nose.

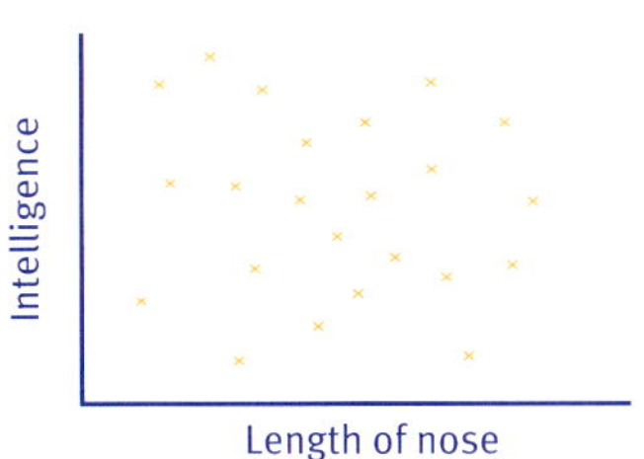

EXAM TIP

The closer the points are to making a straight line, the stronger the correlation.

Sequences

Learn to recognise these special sequences:

Even numbers:	2, 4, 6, 8, 10, 12, 14, 16, 18, 20, …
Odd numbers:	1, 3, 5, 7, 9, 11, 13, 15, 17, 19, …
Square numbers	1, 4, 9, 16, 25, 36, 49, 64, 81, 100, …
Cube numbers	1, 8, 27, 64, 125, 216, 343, 512, 729, …
Triangular numbers	1, 3, 6, 10, 15, 21, 28, 36, 45, 55, …

The nth term for each is:

Even numbers:	$2n$
Odd numbers:	$2n - 1$
Square numbers	n^2
Cube numbers	n^3
Triangular numbers	$\frac{1}{2}n(n + 1)$

For other sequences find the difference between the terms.

E.g.

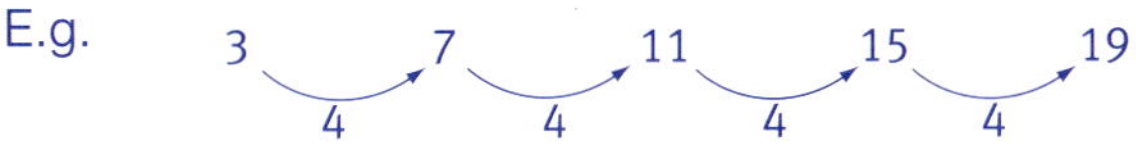

The nth term for this pattern is $4n - 1$.

SEE ALSO Square numbers, Cube numbers, *n*th term

Significant figures

The first (or most) significant figure of a number is the first digit (from the left) that isn't a zero.

The first significant figure in each of these numbers is in bold:

3 759 000   **4**.809   0.**7**23 194   0.000 **6**25

The digits to the right of the first significant figure are the second, third, fourth significant figures, etc. whether they are zero or not.

1st 2nd 3rd 4th …
3704.68

1st 2nd 3rd 4th …
0.000 **6**205

SEE ALSO Rounding

Similarity

Shapes that have been made larger or smaller but have not changed shape are known as **similar**. The angles are the same and their sides are in the same proportion or ratio.

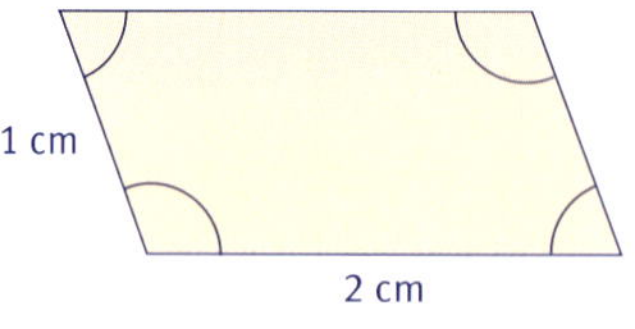

SEE ALSO Scale factor, Transformations

Simplifying

1 Collect together all the terms that are the same. Treat letters, like g and $3f$, separately from numbers, e.g. 6 and 2.

E.g. $g + 3g - f + 6 + 4f - 2 - 2g + f$

$= 2g + 4f + 4$

Watch out for negative signs!

2 If you can, put any brackets back in to simplify further.

E.g. $2g + 4f + 4$

$= 2(g + 2f + 2)$

EXAM TIP

If simplifying expressions such as $12x^2 + 3x + 6$, treat x^2 and x separately. They cannot be grouped together. $12x^2 + 3x + 6 = 3(4x^2 + x + 2)$

SEE ALSO Algebraic expressions, Brackets, Factorising

Simultaneous equations

When solving simultaneous equations, you are trying to find the solutions that two or more equations have in common.

There are several different ways to solve simultaneous equations.

E.g. $x + y = 11$

$2x - y = 4$

Elimination method

1 Try to add or subtract the equations if you can, to eliminate one of the letters.

$x + y = 11$

$2x - y = 4$ Add to eliminate y

$\mathbf{3x = 15}$

So $x = 5$.

2 Once you know the value of one letter, put it into one of the equations.

$x + y = 11$

If x is 5, $5 + y = 11$.

So $y = 6$.

Solutions: $x = 5$, $y = 6$

Continued overleaf

Substitution method

1 Rearrange one equation to read '$y = \dots$' or '$x = \dots$'.

$x + y = 11$

so $y = 11 - x$

2 Substitute this into the other equation.

$2x - y = 4$

$2x - (11 - x) = 4$

Simplify $3x - 11 = 4$

And rearrange $3x = 15$

So $x = 5$

3 Once you know the value of one letter, put it into one of the equations.

$x + y = 11$

If x is 5, $5 + y = 11$. So $y = 6$. Solutions: $x = 5$, $y = 6$

Graph method

Plot the two lines on the same graph and see where they cross.

SEE ALSO Linear graphs

Square numbers

Square numbers (sometimes called squared numbers) are made by multiplying one number by itself.

E.g.

1×1	2×2	3×3	4×4	5×5	6×6	7×7	8×8	9×9	10×10
1	**4**	**9**	**16**	**25**	**36**	**49**	**64**	**81**	**100 ...**

They are called square numbers because they are the sequence of areas of squares.

SEE ALSO Cube numbers, Sequences, *n*th term

Squares and square roots

To square a number (^{2}), we multiply it by itself.

We can do the opposite by using square root ($\sqrt{}$). Using this we can find which number has been squared.

Squaring a number, e.g. 7 or 2.6

$7^2 = 7 \times 7 = 49$ $2.6^2 = 2.6 \times 2.6 = 6.76$

Find the square root, e.g. of 49 or 6.76

$\sqrt{49} = 7$
because 7×7 is 49

$\sqrt{6.76} = 2.6$
because 2.6×2.6 is 6.76

On your calculator, look for a key marked x^2 or $\sqrt{}$. Sometimes these are the same key, so you may have to use 'inv' or 'shift' for one of them.

SEE ALSO Pythagoras' Theorem

Standard form

Standard form is used to write very large numbers or very small numbers in a simpler way. A number in standard form looks like this:

Ten 'to the power' 8

4.31×10^8

The number before the decimal point must be between 1 and 9.

Substitution

Substitute the numbers you have been given for the letters in a formula.

E.g. $z = 3x + \frac{1}{2}y$ Find z if $x = 5$ and $y = 4$.

$z = 3x + \frac{1}{2}y$

3×5 $\frac{1}{2}$ of 4 Substitute 5 and 4 for the letters.

$z = 15 + 2$ Work out the answer!

$z = 17$

Remember that $3x$ means $3 \times x$ or 3 lots of x.
Substitution can be used to solve simultaneous equations.

SEE ALSO Formula, Equations, Linear equations, Simultaneous equations

Surface area

To find the surface area of a cuboid, find the area of pairs of opposite faces separately.

E.g.

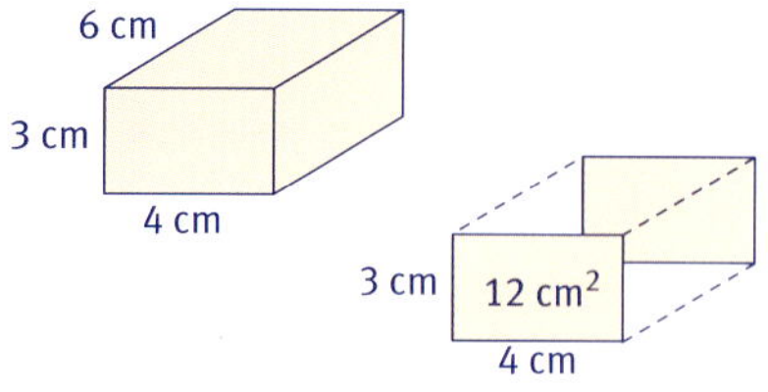

Two faces of 12 cm^2 $2 \times 12 = 24$ cm^2
Two faces of 24 cm^2 $2 \times 24 = 48$ cm^2
Two faces of 18 cm^2 $2 \times 18 = 36$ cm^2

Surface area = 108 cm^2

SEE ALSO Area

Time

60 seconds = 1 minute 24 hours = 1 day
60 minutes = 1 hour 7 days = 1 week
1 year = 52 weeks = 365 (or 366) days = 12 months
10 years = 1 decade 100 years = 1 century 1000 years = 1 millennium

1 Change 453 minutes to hours and minutes.
*How many 60s in **453**?* $7 \times 60 = 420$
453 is 33 more than 420.
So **453** minutes = 7 hours and 33 minutes.

2 A plane took off at 18:25 and landed at 21:10. How long was the journey?
Split this time into smaller periods:
18:25 → 19:00 → 21:00 → 21:10
35 minutes *2 hours* *10 minutes*
Journey time = 2 hours 45 minutes.

EXAM TIP

In the 12-hour clock: a.m. = midnight to midday; p.m. = midday to midnight.

Transformations

A transformation is a way of moving or changing a shape.
There are four main types of transformation.

1 Reflection

2 Rotation (turning)

3 Translation (sliding)

4 Enlargement (making larger or smaller)

E.g. In the diagram, Shape A has been changed to the other shapes by the transformations described.

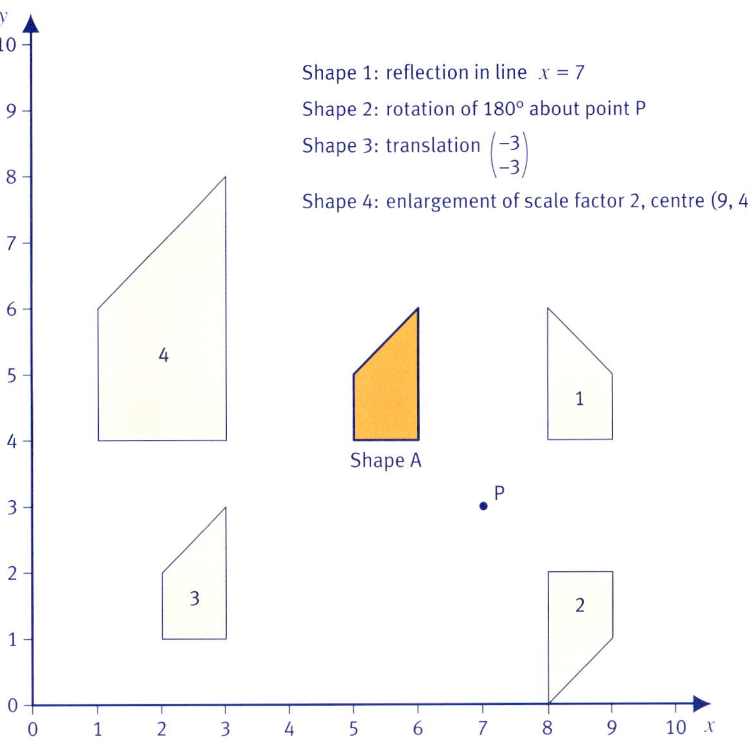

SEE ALSO Reflective symmetry, Rotational symmetry, Scale factor

Tree diagrams

Tree diagrams can be used to find probabilities.
For example, six socks are in a drawer. Four are black and two are white. Sam picks one sock and then a second without looking. What is the probability that he picks two white socks?

Sam's first pick
Probability (P) of picking:
a white = $^2\!/_6$
a black = $^4\!/_6$

Sam's second pick
Probabilities will depend on what he has picked on the first go.

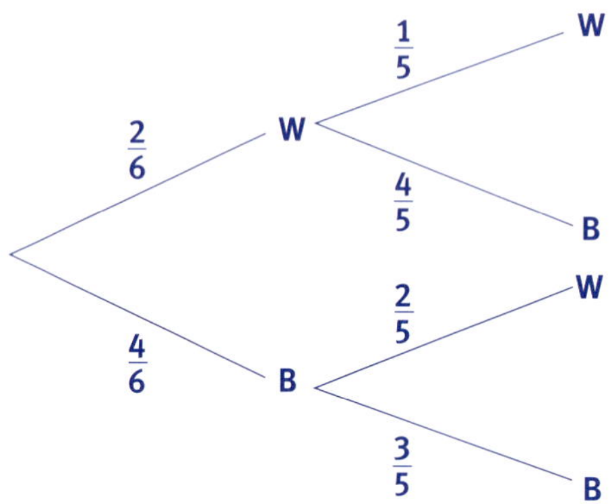

$$\frac{2}{6} \times \frac{1}{5} = \frac{2}{30} = \frac{1}{15}$$

$$\frac{2}{6} \times \frac{4}{5} = \frac{8}{30} = \frac{4}{15}$$

$$\frac{4}{6} \times \frac{2}{5} = \frac{8}{30} = \frac{4}{15}$$

$$\frac{4}{6} \times \frac{3}{5} = \frac{12}{30} = \frac{6}{15}$$

To find the probability (P) of picking two whites, follow the tree, from left to right, to W and then W. Write the two probabilities down and **multiply** them together.

Probability (P) that Sam picks two whites = $\frac{2}{6} \times \frac{1}{5} = \frac{2}{30} = \frac{1}{15}$.

Notice that all the probabilities for every possible outcome **total 1**.

$$\frac{1}{15} + \frac{4}{15} + \frac{4}{15} + \frac{6}{15} = \frac{15}{15} = 1$$

SEE ALSO Probability, Fractions

Trial and improvement

Trial and improvement can be used to solve a problem.
E.g. Find the value of x if $x^2 - x + 1 = \mathbf{1.24}$.
Draw a table, like this. Try larger and smaller values of x.

Choose a value for x to start. You want the answer in this column to be **1.24**.

x	x^2	$x^2 - x$	$x^2 - x + 1$	
1	1	0	1	too small (x must be more than 1)
2	4	2	3	too large (x must be less than 2)
1.5	2.25	0.75	1.75	too large (x must be less than 1.5)
1.1	1.21	0.11	1.11	too small (x must be more than 1.1)
1.3	1.69	0.39	1.39	too large (x must be less than 1.3)
1.2	1.44	0.24	1.24	correct! (x must be 1.2)

Triangles

Right-angled triangles have one angle of 90°.

Obtuse-angled triangles have one angle greater than 90°.

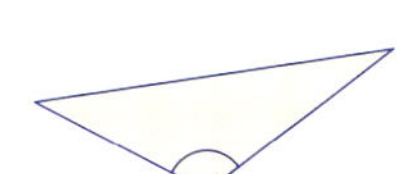

Any triangle is either equilateral, isosceles or scalene.

Equilateral triangles have three sides the same length and three equal angles. They are the only regular triangles.

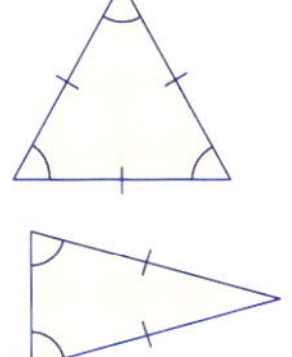

Isosceles triangles have two sides the same and two equal angles.

Scalene triangles have no sides of the same length and no equal angles.

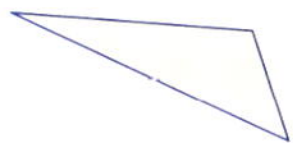

SEE ALSO Interior and exterior angles, Regular polygons, Pythagoras' Theorem

Volume

The volume of an object is the amount of space it takes up.

Cuboid

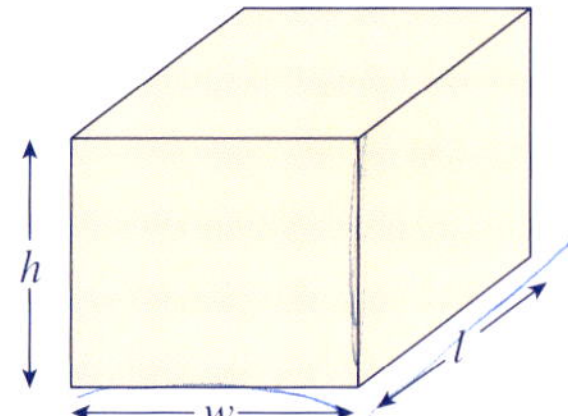

Volume = length × width × height
$V = l \times w \times h$

Prisms
Volume = area of end face (orange face) × length

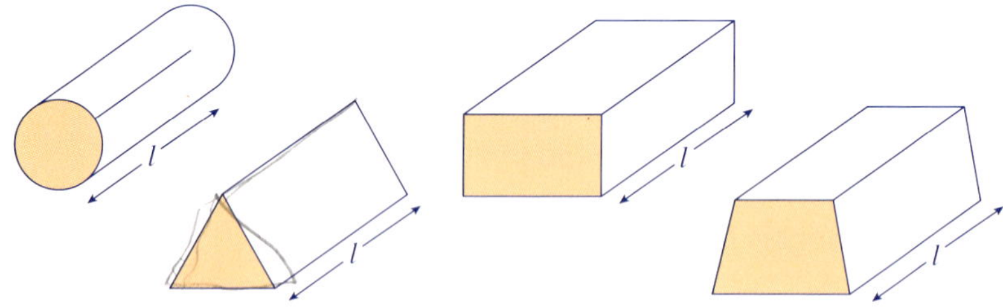

EXAM TIP

Remember that volume is expressed as e.g. cm^3 or m^3.

SEE ALSO Area, Circles

Weight

Weight is a measure of how heavy an object is. It is the force of gravity acting upon something and is measured in **newtons**. Grams and kilograms are more correctly units of mass.

SEE ALSO Mass